First Facts

Community Helpers at Work

A Day in the Life of a
Farmer

by Heather Adamson

Consultants:
The Staff of the
National Farmers Union
Aurora, Colorado

Capstone
press

Mankato, Minnesota

First Facts is published by Capstone Press
151 Good Counsel Drive, P.O. Box 669, Mankato, Minnesota 56002
http://www.capstone-press.com

Library of Congress Cataloging-in-Publication Data
Adamson, Heather, 1974–
    A day in the life of a farmer/by Heather Adamson.
    v. cm.—(First facts: Community helpers at work)
    Includes bibliographical references and index.
    Contents: When do farmers start their days?—What do farm animals eat?—Why are
there so many buildings on a farm?—Do farmers work by themselves?—What does a
combine do?—Who takes care of farm machines?—What happens to the corn that is
harvested?—Where do farmers live?
    ISBN 0-7368-2283-6 (hardcover)
    1. Farmers—Juvenile literature. 2. Agriculture—Vocational guidance—Juvenile
literature. [1. Farmers. 2. Farm life. 3. Occupations.] I. Title. II. Series.
S519 .A32 2004
630′ .92—dc21
                                                                                    2002155825

Credits
Jennifer Schonborn, series and book designer; Gary Sundermeyer, photographer;
    Eric Kudalis, product planning editor

Artistic Effects
Ingram Publishing; PhotoDisc

Capstone Press thanks farmers Dave Barton, Dale Berndt, and James Scheurer for the use of
    their farms and equipment in the photographing of this book.

1 2 3 4 5 6 08 07 06 05 04 03

Table of Contents

When do farmers start their days?

Farmers start their days very early. Every day, Farmer Dave gets up while it is still dark. He puts on his coat and walks to the dairy barn. He pulls on his gloves to milk the cows. Farmer Dave will milk the cows again in the evening.

Fun Fact:
One cow can produce up to 8 gallons (30 liters) of milk per day.

5:00 in the morning

5

What do farm animals eat?

Many farm animals eat food grown on the farm. Farmer Dave feeds his cows a mix of hay and corn. He also gives all the farm animals vitamins to keep them healthy.

6:00 in the morning

Why are there so many buildings on a farm?

 Fun Fact:

U.S. farms produced more than 9 billion bushels (300 million cubic meters) of corn in 2002.

Farms have many kinds of buildings and
bins. Some buildings hold animals. Bins and
silos store grains. Many farms also have
sheds to protect their machines. Dave keeps
tools in his red barn. He needs to get a
wrench to fix one of the tractors.

9

Do farmers work by themselves?

Farmers need help to do their jobs. Families or neighbors sometimes work together. Since it is a weekend, Dave's children help feed the animals. Farmer Dave has hired an extra worker to help with the harvesting.

10:00 in the
morning

What does a combine do?

Farmers use a combine to harvest crops.
The combine cuts down the cornstalks.

11:00 in the
morning

Then, it separates the kernels from the corn cobs. Dave parks the tractor and wagon beside the combine. The combine unloads the corn into the wagon.

Who takes care of farm machines?

Farmers must learn how to keep their machines running well. Over the noon hour, Dave greases the engine. He cleans dust out of the combine's hopper. He takes care of his machines so they will last longer.

Fun Fact:

New farm machines use GPS (global positioning satellite) systems. Farmers can make maps of fields while they are d

12:00 in the afternoon

15

3:30 in the
afternoon

16

What happens to the corn that is harvested?

Some farmers sell their corn to companies that make food for supermarkets. Farmer Dave uses his corn to feed his animals. An auger lifts the corn to the top of the bin. The corn will stay fresh in the bins and silos all winter.

17

Where do farmers live?

Farmers usually live on their farms. Farmer Dave parks his tractor in the shed. After milking the cows again, he walks to the house to clean up. Then, he sits down to eat with his family. It is good to be home.

Fun Fact:
The average American drinks about 24 gallons (91 liters) of milk each year.

6:30 in the
evening

Amazing But True!

Some cows eat cereal and potato chips. Farmers buy leftover cereal and potato chips from factories. The farmers mix it in with the cows' usual meals of hay, corn, and grass.

Wagons
pulled behind a tractor and used for hauling

Oversized Tire
large, rear tires move through mud

Door

Cab

Lights

Hat

Boots

21

Glossary

auger (AW-ger)—a device that moves loose material; farmers use augers to lift corn and other grains into wagons, bins, and silos.

combine (KOM-bine)—a machine that is used to harvest corn and other grains

crop (KROP)—a plant grown in large amounts that is often used for food

silo (SYE-loh)—a tall, round tower used to store food for farm animals

vitamin (VYE-tuh-min)—a healthy part of food; farm animals are fed extra vitamins to help them grow large and strong.

wrench (RENCH)—a tool for tightening and loosening nuts or bolts

Read More

Flanagan, Alice K. *Farmers.* Community Workers. Minneapolis: Compass Point Books, 2003.

Klingel, Cynthia Fitterer. *Farmers.* Wonder Books. Chanhassen, Minn.: Child's World, 2002.

Internet Sites

Do you want to find out more about farmers? Let FactHound, our fact-finding hound dog, do the research for you!

Here's how:
1. Visit *www.facthound.com*
2. Type in the **Book ID** number: 0736822836
3. Click on **FETCH IT**.

FactHound will fetch Internet sites picked by our editors just for you!

Index